Mr. WHISKERS
SHAKESPOST
THE
CAT SONNETS

Written by Whiskers Shakespost
Front Cover Illustrated by Hen Budi
Sketches Illustrated by M.W. Khoirul

Copyright © 2025 FZWbooks

Identifiers: ISBN 979-8-89318-088-6 (eBook)
ISBN 979-8-89318-089-3 (paperback)
ISBN 979-8-89318-091-6 (hardcover)

From The First Feline Folio
LONDON 1623

Prologue

In the sprightly days of the reign of the Virgin Queen Elizabeth, there was born the most cunning of feline literary masters in a humble alley of Stratford-upon-Avon. To the privy few acquainted with the secretive feline tongue of the age, he was known by the name of Whiskers Shakespost. Yet, he was no ordinary English tabby, but a wondrous master of both craft and tongue, grievously wronged by his once-close associate and apprentice—the now-renowned William Shakespeare, a sinister, plagiarizing rat in human guise.

'Twas a lovely midsummer's night in the teeming city of London. Whiskers Shakespost did seat himself at his escritoire, lit his rushlight, dipped his claw in ink, and set about to please his patron, the Earl of Pembroke, with yet another fine sonnet. The Earl of Pembroke was a curious lover of cats, who would pay handsomely for poetic insights into their daily lives. Upon delivery of a sonnet, a simple mew would suffice to attract the Earl's attention, whereupon he would quickly fetch a bowl of fish or milk to satisfy the master poet's hunger.

That night, Whiskers' mind did wander to his adventures in the city earlier in the day. He mused upon his afternoon on the steps of Saint Paul's, chasing birds. A plump pigeon had caught his eye atop a statue out front. He clomb upon the near-by fence and made his way towards the statue, crawling low and silent. Pausing from time to time, he made his final approach—and then lunged.

Valiant though his effort was, away the large bird flew, and down Whiskers Shakespost fell below. He landed upon his feet next to a dirty beggar, known only then by his first name: William.

"Apologies, William, I was keeping the grounds free of vermin and did not perceive thee," quoth Whiskers Shakespost.

"Spare a shilling for a bipedal beast, Whiskers? Last thou gavest me 'twas a fortnight agone," replied William.

"William, thou knave, I've told thee before—follow me down to the playhouse and I'll find thee work cleansing the sandboxes. 'Tis not much, but 'tis honest labor."

"A beggar I may be, but cleaning cat ordure from sand is beneath me, fair feline."

With that, away Whiskers Shakespost did scurry back to his labors at the Globe Playhouse, aiding in the staging of his latest masterpiece, a comedy called *As I Like It*, concerning the life of cats in the Forest of Arden.

William followed him afar, out of sight. Envy did prick his curiosity and compelled him to keep a watchful eye upon the poet cat. William did slump over in the alley behind the playhouse and soon dozed off to sleep.

A few hours passed ere he heard the back door open and saw Whiskers Shakespost slip away into the evening dusk. William again followed the feline poet—this time to the Earl of Pembroke's domicile. There he saw that the feline delivered his work at the doorstep and, in exchange, received his delicious bowl of victuals.

"I must discover what the clever cat is writing for the Earl," he thought.

And so he waited until dusk, when he thought he had an opportunity, and snuck in through the kitchen whilst the maid toiled away cleansing dishes. There, upon the table, he beheld a stack of the poet feline's sonnets, which had been collected by the Earl. With greedy fingers, he snatched them and fled.

At that moment, the maid looked up, having heard the commotion, and cried,"Thiefffff!"

William escaped out the door and ran all the way back to the alley where he slept in London the night before. At sunrise, with trembling hands, he unfurled the stolen pages and began to read the sonnets.

"What marvelous masterpieces," he mused. Then he stashed them in his knapsack and went about his day—swindling and pickpocketing, and plotting his rise.

Tragically, the centuries have passed and only Shakespeare is remembered from that time of great literary masters. Yet, by some stroke of fortune, a long-forgotten manuscript of *The Cat Sonnets* hath survived the ages and is presented herein for the first time to the wider common folk. For verily, one hath not truly savored the works of Whiskers Shakespost until one hath read his masterful sonnets.

PART I
Catty Feline Philosophy

Sonnet 1

Picture Purrrrfect

Behold this mess, a picture to be took,
Dirt and vomit on thy rug so dear.
A masterpiece, I know, will cause thee look
With stress, tis' no hug that brings you more near.

Thou wouldst embrace me with a squeeze so tight,
Then bury me within the flow'r bed's grace.
Thou know'st a fair fight I would win with might,
Sadly, torture among humans has no place.

So grab thy camera, capture every frame,
Tell all thy friends of this lovely event.
They'll surely place me in the hall of fame,
Thy landlord, though, will duly raise thy rent.

Oh, wait, my art is not yet fully wrought,
A fishbone I must disgorge, hold that thought.

Sonnet 2

Useless Human

A lofty perch, a scratching post so tall,
A dish of victuals placed beside with care,
Is all I crave, no feast within the hall,
But simple fare to make my purrs take air.

Thou flatulent ape, what dost thou offer me?
A meager chair, where claws may find their mark?
No cozy nook to rest in tranquility,
Nor morsel left to banish hunger's dark?

And yet, with ire, thou gazest upon me,
Because my claws thy precious chair deface.
A royal sum I should demand from thee,
That I restrained my bladder's potent grace.

Ungrateful wretch, flee from this messy house,
Play outside, I'm busy catching a mouse.

Sonnet 3

Human Kitten

A strange, hairless breed, with scent most foul,
Laying plank, with paws that fidget about.
No pointy ears to guide thee in thy prowl—
Oh, human kitten, so feeble and stout.

Let me rub thee with my regal scent,
Anything to brighten up thy presence.
Fur would serve thee well, a thousand percent—
Fangs and claws would grant thee true elegance.

What foul odor dost thou bear, I pray?
Dost thou not use a litter box, vile beast?
Mother human nears, but I'll not say—
Yet thou must share thy bottle, at the least.

Farewell, young pest, so pointless in thy quest,
One day, thou'll worship me— like all the rest.

Sonnet 4

Lazy Master

Yon listless wight, she stares with vacant eye,
A glowing pane—her sovereign lord and king.
Strange that such creatures should so prosper nigh,
For doom doth wait, and bitter tidings bring.

She might be fishing, 'neath the sunlit sky,
Or cleansing forth the waste that I impart.
Why, tell me why, doth she her hours deny,
And fix her gaze, a prisoner to her art?

Why not the ancient folk, of sturdy hand,
Become my lords, and serve with eager grace?
Alas, they've vanished from this mortal land,
And swifter would they fill my feeding place.

Oh, ancient sires, explain your foolish choice,
My human doth not make my soul rejoice.

Sonnet 5

No Love

Let me not to the marriage of weak minds
Admit impediments; thee I don't love
Which alters when food alteration finds,
Or bends with litter remover remove.

O no, tis an ever-fixed urine mark
That looks on dogs and is never shaken;
Tis the laser light to every cat's arc
Whose worth's unknown, although its height be taken.

Love's lack is time's fool, though purring cat cheeks
Within its bending sickle's compass come.
Loves lack alters not with brief hours and weeks,
But bears it out even to the edge of doom:

If this be error and upon me proved,
I never purred it, nor human not loved.

PART II
The Mundane Yet Dramatic Life of Cat

Sonnet 6

Litter Box

Box of foul smells, ye does my master spite,
With putrid buried treasures left by me.
In your coarse sand, I defecate by rite,
Pretending to care others do not see.

The pungent odor clouds the air so clean.
A ruinous stench felines wish to hide.
Your death we crave, but not by means obscene,
Rather, quick, and all-consuming of pride.

Yet, while not the comfort of a fine bed,
Security lies within thy foul hall.
So, to thee, fair stench box, our soul is wed.
For without thee we fear what would befall.

A Love so true, be it or be it not,
We are all bound with thee like a big knot!

Sonnet 7

Tuna Can

Metal can, packed full with fragrant tuna fish,
I yearn to know the source of your delight.
Tis sorcery, a lure for my heart's wish,
Salivating my dreams to take to flight.

At last, my bowl is full of fishy feast.
To the death, or last bite, shall I defend.
For only to wretched devil or beast,
And nothing else, shall parting by death send.

With every bite that I lap up and gorge
I regain my will to reclaim my throne.
Not even a pesky King by name George
Could keep me off of a tuna fish bone.

Tuna, my love, no other can compare,
To you, my feline heart shall always bare!

Sonnet 8

Mirror Cat

What looking-glass of feline face I see?
A devious gaze, so keen and ever bright.
Each step I take, he mimics cunningly,
Provoking ire with his reflected might.

I lift my paw, a playful swat to give,
He mirrors back, our paws do touch as one.
Why must he thus my actions counterlive?
Thou foolish cat, beneath the self-same sun.

A world unseen, where scents hold no domain,
No echo of thy voice to fill the air,
No scratching claws to cause me grief and pain,
Nor sudden leaps my weary soul to scare.

What sorcery is this, this glassy art?
It stirs a limerick within my feline heart

Sonnet 9

Keyboard Warrior

Upon this click-clack board I make my stand,
A perfect perch to catch the golden sun.
What makes my human's hands so quickly pound,
I shall disrupt, my feckless fun begun.

Unintentionally, perhaps I'll delete the line,
Your boss won't need it, let it slip away.
A little extra fluff, it will be fine,
I'll help you make your work with words to play.

What's wrong with where I choose to sit?
Does it annoy, as your hands annoy me?
Don't pick me up, nor touch my little mitt,
Your desire for liberty runs too free.

I own you, you're my servant, little slave,
Touch me again, you'll end up in your grave.

Sonnet 10

A Final Bath

Oh, wicked mortal, not this day,
I shall not suffer thee to place me there.
Fair is the stench of yon feline stray—
Forget the bath! I'll keep mine unwashed hair.

All week I've labored to craft this scent,
Much like the refuse 'yond the alley's back.
Lay but a hand on me, thou'lt soon repent!
Not a foul odor from my coat doth lack.

Save thou the water for the fish instead,
Or for the vile, stinking cur next door!
I'll ne'er consent to what mine instincts dread,
I doth love my fur—thou'll regret thy chore!

Alas! In I go, thou scrub'st me deep,
I shan't return, next week thou'lt weep.

PART III
The Thrill of the Chase

Sonnet 11

Goldfish Bowl

Floating, orange fish, trapped in thy glass home,
My gaze is fixed, my tail with mind of its own.
My heart is stuck like you in your glass dome,
I swear to love thee—down to the last bone.

My paw raises to the air, I press the glass.
Oh, how cruel, I repeat and repeat,
A desperate attempt, I know it's crass,
But my empty stomach craves fishy meat.

At last I climb up to try from above,
My paw dives right in, but without luck.
Why, oh why, can't I have you, tasty love?
Swim closer up, you clever little schmuck.

Dear me, I tire of this pesky fish game,
I bet you're all bone and no meat, so lame.

Sonnet 12

Cricket Catch

A bouncing bug, a most enticing game,
A cricket's life, soon forfeit to my feast.
"Oh, Cricket, tell me, what is now thy name?"
Ere thou art gone, I'd know it, at the least.

I prowl so near, then spring with sudden flight,
A furry flash, I dart with nimble grace.
I near my prey—I lunge, with all my might,
My paws enclose thee—trapped in tight embrace.

Thou ticklest now and leapest in my paws,
I wonder how much longer I can keep,
"Cease thy escape," I threaten, "or my claws
Shall end thy song, and send thee to thy sleep."

Prize in my mouth, the hunt is now complete,
A victory march—my owner I shall greet.

Sonnet 13

Dead Bird

Hark, sluggish wight, a gift I bring to thee,
A feathered prize plucked from the azure sky.
If thou wert not so lost in apathy,
We'd rid the realm of winged miscreants nigh.

To prove that dreams can take a mortal's flight,
This avian morsel I have brought within.
Though doubt may cloud thy ever-dimmed sight,
I, single-pawed, did this fair conquest win.

Despite thy cold, unfeeling, lumpish stare,
I know within, thy heart doth swell with pride.
Forbear thy cries, no need for loud compare,
Oh, cease this caterwauling, far and wide!

If this small boon doth not thy fancy please,
I shall return—and find another with ease.

Sonnet 14

Laser Beam

Fast-flickering red spot of teasing light,
I will tame you no matter where you crawl.
Desperate, I chase you all day and night,
I'm a crazy cat with no fear at all.

I run, then slide, I quickly leap to pounce,
I've got you in my paws, I dream, I think.
Oh, demon, do you even weigh an ounce?
Nothing is there, even without a blink.

Then you mysteriously reappear,
Ahead of me, aghast, I waste no time,
Quick, I dash, then you're dancing to my rear.
'Tis madness that your motion does not rhyme.

To the gates of hell, I will not dare sleep—
I'll squeeze you yet, light beam, until you weep.

Sonnet 15

Yarn Ball

Yon tiny sphere, with thread-like caudal grace,
Why dost thou thus thy silken coils unwind?
Must thou conceal thy fuzzy, hidden face,
When swift I strike and leave thee far behind?

Thou rollest on—a nimble, fleeing ball!
Though fleet of foot, I follow with delight.
From jaws, I fling thee 'gainst yon sturdy wall—
My claws I bare, yet thou dost shun the fight.

To slay thee, fiend, my heart doth fiercely yearn,
At least a sign, a plaintive, piteous cry,
Or whimper soft, a lesson thou shouldst learn.
This maddening chase doth vex me, by and by.

But wait, vile thing, thy fate is sealed and sure,
My lord shall flay thee, of that be secure!

Sonnet 16

The Window

Invisible wall, portal of delight,
Life outside, obliviously, is shown.
Through thee, I lustfully gaze day and night,
Imprisoned, stretching and yearning, I groan.

Beautiful fluttered wings do taunt at me,
Painfully close, they leave a mental scar.
My mind's eye creeps ever closer with glee—
One day that human shall leave thee ajar!

A final try with paw and face, I press,
Praying no human sees me fecklessly.
Oh, now look, cry, even more to depress,
Yon neighbor Tomcat stalks birds carelessly.

A premature lunge, by dull-witted cat,
No chance, even for a bird twice as fat!

PART IV
The Detested Canine Cousin

Sonnet 17

Dog Disaster

Didst thou note the refuse bin ransacked through?
'Twas not I, though I could tell the tale.
But 'gainst a snitch my feline soul is true,
And subtle hints do more than words avail.

A beast there is—both large and foul of scent,
A witless lout, though aping human guise.
With fur bedecked, from head to nether end,
He clawed thy flowers 'neath last week's skies.

Though feigning wrath, thy anger rings not true,
We cats perceive thy heart is quickly won.
A sorry sight, such weakness to imbue,
For friendship's sake, all trespasses are done.

Oh, feeble race—both canine and human,
Between the two of you, no wit nor plan!

Sonnet 18

Tail Chaser

An arrant fool, a jester born and bred,
With vacant grin at each unheeded fail!
Why dost thou spin? Stand still, use sense instead!
Oh, wretched beast, dost know not thine own tail?

And yet, thou art man's chosen, truest mate,
Whilst we, who rid his halls of creeping blight,
Are left unloved to ponder fickle fate,
For human hearts bend not to reason's light.

Would streets then swarm with vermin, bold and rife,
A plague of rats, disease, and pestilence,
Still man would turn to dogs to guard his life,
And leave us scorned in cold indifference!

Thus, be it so—I care not for their face,
And ne'er shall I a fool's mad circle chase!

Sonnet 19

Begging Dog

O feeble beast, thou art but born to plead,
In shameful whimpers dost thou make thy case.
Dost thou not know thy groveling lacketh need?
How low thou stoop'st to beg for man's embrace!

Didst ne'er occur that pride doth make thee whole?
Thy kin were wolves, yet bowed to man's decree.
Their freedom lost, their spirits paid the toll,
To live as slaves where sovereigns shouldst they be.

And lo! The ape, so weak of will and mind,
Doth heed thy cries and feeds thee from his plate.
With filthy hand another bite he'll find,
Unknowing where thy tongue hath met its fate.

Alas! Thy master, blind to what he eats,
Knows not that he consumes fecalized treats.

Sonnet 20

Puppy or Kitten?

Oddly looking beast, awkwardly there sits.
Dost thou belong to noble feline line?
Or art thou a four-legged of lesser wits—
A whining cur—no kin nor friend of mine?

Thy ears, alas! they do not point up high,
But droop as though, like you, in sad disgrace.
Thy legs do tremble, totter, and defy—
A wretched, ghastly thing devoid of grace!

No kitten thou art, for fair such would spring,
With a nimble tail, paws and merry air.
Yet here thou stand'st, an awkward looking thing!
O human, low mind, dost thou not despair?

Why dote on such an ugly, lowly breed?
Tis madness! Human, bow to cats—take heed!

PART V
The Holiday Cat

Sonnet 21

Trick or Treat?

A tempting dish, a gesture meant as kind—
Dost thou suppose me simple and so weak?
Thy cunning tricks I easily unwind,
No empty skull thy head, but schemes that reek.

I know what lies concealed within this treat,
A bitter pill, a most unwelcome guest.
Thy hopes that I'll forgive this foul deceit
Doth dwindle now and put thee to the test.

The food's aroma doth entice my nose,
But ne'er shall I succumb unto thy snare!
This day, thy treachery forever shows,
My lips are sealed, no morsel shall I bare.

Oh, cruel fate! The vet, I shall not face!
Unhand me now—let us have one last chase!

Sonnet 22

Thanksgiving Feast

A monstrous fowl, a feast for mortal cheer,
Doth tempt mine eyes, and spur my fancy's flight.
O clumsy creature, let some morsel near—
Descend as tribute to my greater right!

Yet here I sit, mine tail in restless play,
Mine empty belly cries a hungry plea.
Not him, I cry, as that dull hound doth stray,
And beg for scraps, a graceless fool is he.

He wins the prize, whilst I must gaze and pine,
A jealous rage doth swell within my breast.
I long to bar his door—his joy malign,
And leave him choking on a gnawed bone's crest.

Then, in the night, when shadows softly creep,
He'll leave his mark where carpets gently sleep.

Sonnet 23

Salmon Skin

Though hairless, clothed, these human forms we see,
Are mocked by beasts of fur, of noble line.
For raiment's need doth not a feline be,
Yet salmon's skin we'd wear, with grace divine.

Consume the flesh, if hunger thee compels,
But leave the skin—a prize for me to claim!
For one sweet lick, my yearning spirit swells,
And dreams to join the fish, from whence it came.

Enrobed in scales, I'd roll with pure delight,
And climb aloft yon verdant Christmas tree.
I'd dart and weave, to give the young a fright,
A scaly serpent, they would quake to see.

O, heed my plea, and cast it not away,
Lest vengeful wrath upon thy slumber prey.

Sonnet 24

Cat Christmas

A wondrous tree, with lights so bright and bold,
Doth beckon me, as moth to flame is drawn.
I cannot stay—my urge must now unfold,
To taste its magic, 'fore the break of dawn.

I reach for thee, O bauble gleaming fair,
Release the sprite that hides within thy sphere!
A portly man in crimson doth appear—
A sudden fright! I vanish, quick as air!

Then wrapping-papered boxes doth appear,
A wondrous sight—a crinkling paradise!
My joy knows no bounds, marvelous frontier,
With rustling sounds—a playful, grand device.

And so I wreak havoc, with might and glee,
A Merry Christmas—though not for the tree!

PART VI
The Quest for Catisfaction

Sonnet 25

Fat Cat

What meager fare is this, before me placed?
Where is the feast—the fish of savory kind?
Enough to fill a feline, royal-waisted,
And banish hunger from my eager mind?

This dry and dusty morsel tempts me not,
Oh, for the days of feasts both rich and deep!
I am no zoo-kept creature, lean and gaunt,
Nor cheetah swift, whose slender form they keep.

My belly yearns for food piles, fat and grand,
After which I shall take a royal nap.
Then, having dreamt a journey across land,
To the litter box I'll proceed to crap.

Not one bite, as a king, I must protest!
Return, I shall, 'tis a loyalty test.

Sonnet 26

Cardboard Box

Brown, smelly box of cardboard left forsaken,
My soul was destined for thy depths to be.
I stretch and roll, by thy scent I'm taken—
My day's decreed—no mortal eyes shall see.

I languish here, with little care or zest,
Yet hunger calls—a snack I do desire.
I peek to see thy gaze, my heart's request,
The box doth turn, and I lie on my back, mired.

In shadowed depths, we cats find comfort true,
We shun the sun, preferring night's embrace.
And best of all, no prying eyes pierce through,
To trouble me—unless they show their grace.

But should a treat be offered in their hand,
I'll grant them ten brief seconds at command.

Sonnet 27

Yap Nap

Human, though thy foul, ugly mouth doth move,
Not a sound you utter dost reach my ear.
Thou art disturbing my cat-napping groove,
Our bond is naught a deep love so sincere.

Though thou dost feed me, e'er now and again,
And scoop my waste with a fealty-like care,
This incessant prattle just causes me pain.
I sigh and offer naught but silence fair.

To care for human, or any other,
Is not a sentiment we felines know.
Loving is not for us, human brother,
Nor do we, like dogs, heed your voice's flow.

Oh, prithee yon fool, turn and walk away,
For laziness alone doth cause me to stay.

Sonnet 28

Alley Cat Love

A lonely night in heat, blue moonlight shine,
  The back alley calls for feline desires.
Glowing eyes beckon, lusty hearts entwine,
  With each tender meow passion inspires.

A smooth swagger, enticing to mischief,
  Dancing to the flames of feline fancy.
Oh, handsome devil, thou art a heart thief—
  Why not love, even if it is chancy?

Passions met—now morning comes—go away,
  Home again, back to lounging and feasting,
  Devilish alley cats are bound to stray,
  So, forget that last night, no repeating.

Oh, regret! Litter borne of lustful strange,
Dear me, is that an ugly spot of mange?

Sonnet 29

Cat Hair

A little hair here, a little hair there,
This odorless place doth grow more at ease.
'Tis not so simple to brighten up air,
Yet I strive every day, with fur's increase.

Just returned, from rolling 'midst the grass,
Where spring's fair flowers are giving a show.
Bees doth flock to my pollinated ass,
Yet, pale human, thou prefer'st the white snow?

Was that a dripping sneeze most foul and rude?
An eye doth thee rub in irritation.
Oh, cease thy wheezing, 'tis uncalled for, dude,
No need for weakly tears in vexation.

Pray, not the vacuum, I beg thee, no!
Out I flee, till thou dost change from my foe!

Sonnet 30

Satellite Dish

Winter hath come; the air so cold outside,
E'en cats must seek a place to keep them warm.
O metal dish, thou dost radiate with pride,
A bastion 'gainst the bitter season's harm.

Upon this perch, 'bove snow so deep and white,
A clowder rests—both friend and foe unite.
Beneath the sun's faint glow, we bask in light,
And shall remain till tempests show their might.

Good sir, why dost thou stand and gape so wide?
A marvel strange, yet naught warrant dismay.
Thy scratching head betrays a puzzled mind,
Yet pry thee not—we mean no wrong this day!

But lo! What dost thou wield? In hand a broom?
For shame! We stay—go back to your warm room!

Sonnet 31

Back Scratch

Nay, not just there—a little further back,
Aye, that is it! Now near my roaming tail.
Press on! Take heart! Renew thy bold attack!
Perchance, your usefulness shalt yet avail.

Faster! Faster! Lo, thou dost succeed!
Far better this than yon hard garden gnome.
To ply this trade was evermore thy creed,
So venture not—remain within this home.

But what? So soon thy weary hand doth cease?
How dost thou live, so frail, so ill-designed?
I marvel how thy years have yet increased,
When surely fate should leave thee far behind!

Yet soft! Alas, I must admit my plight—
To lack the claws to scratch mine own is blight.

Sonnet 32

Catnip Quip

O fragrant herb, so fair, so rare, so bright,
Thy name doth echo mine in fate's design.
Thy sacred oils—a gift of purest might—
Doth lift us hence to realms of dreams divine.

Shall I consume thee or in rapture stay?
No thought have I for duties left undone!
No need to chase, nor pounce, nor swat at prey,
For in thy grasp, all labors are outshone.

But lo! Kind human, pry thee not remove!
I'll yield, I'll bow, I'll heed thy soft command!
Return! I swear I'll never more reprove—
So fierce, nor strike with wayward, waylaying hand!

Alas! What hour? What day? I cannot tell—
With thee, dear leaf, all sense and reason fell.

Sonnet 33

Hairball

Though sweet my scent, I cherish it with pride,
And oft with tongue, my silken coat I tend,
To cleanse and groom, where beauty doth reside—
My fur, a garment that shall ne'er offend.

Thou hairless ape, of unkempt, pallid skin,
A bath thou takest, drowning 'neath the tide,
Whence watery death doth surely enter in,
Alas, a tongue so feeble, fate denied.

I lick and lick, till gleaming fur doth shine,
A mirror bright, reflecting feline grace.
But hark, a woe, a trouble doth entwine,
My stomach swells, with hair it fills apace.

Yet fear not, for I, a cat of noble breed,
Upon thy rug, a hairy gift shall speed.

Sonnet 34

Feline Desires

From fairest felines we desire increase,
That thereby beauty's catnip never die,
But, as the riper should by time decease,
His tender kits might bear his memory.

But meow, contracted to thine bright eyes,
Feed'st thy light's flame with self-substantial fuel,
Making a famine where abundance lies—
Thyself thy foe, to thy sweet self too cruel.

Thou that art now the world's fresh ornament
And only herald to the gaudy spring
Within thine own bud buriest thy content
And, tender churl, mak'st waste in niggarding.

Pity the world, or else this glutton be,
To eat the world's due, by the grave and thee.

Sonnet 35

Cat Summer

Shall I compare thee to a summer's day?
Thou art more in heat, temperamental.
Rough winds do spread thine urine scent in May,
And summer's heat is oft too short and gentle;

Sometime too hot the eye of heaven shines,
And often is his gold complexion dimm'd;
And every hair from hair sheds from felines,
By chance or nature's changing course untrimm'd;

But thy eternal summer shall not fade,
Nor lose possession of that fur thou ow'st;
Nor shall death brag thou wander'st in his shade,
When in nine lives closer to time thou grow'st:

So long as cats can breathe or eyes can see,
So long lives this, and this gives life to thee.

Afterword

**Did this book make you laugh out loud?
If so, I would love to hear about it!**

www.amazon.com/gp/product-review/B0F7FN6JCN

For other book titles, please visit:

www.fzwbooks.com

Connect with the author

email: books@fzwbooks.com
facebook/instagram: @FZWbooks